FAMOUS SPY CASES

SPIES AND SPYING

KATE **WALKER** I ELAINE **ARGAET**

This edition first published in 2004 in the United States of America by Smart Apple Media.

Smart Apple Media
1980 Lookout Drive
North Mankato
Minnesota 56003

Library of Congress Cataloging-in-Publication Data

Walker, Kate.
  Famous spy cases / Kate Walker & Elaine Argaet.
  p. cm. — (Spies and spying)

  Includes index.
  Summary: Brief profiles of various spies such as Herbert Murphy, Yoshiko Kawashima, René Duchez, Marita Lorenz, and others.

  ISBN 1-58340-342-6
  1. Spies—Biography—Juvenile literature. [1. Spies.] I. Argaet, Elaine. II. Title. III. Series
  UB270.5.W3396 2003
  327.12'092'2—dc21   2002044619

First Edition
9 8 7 6 5 4 3 2 1

First published in 2003 by
MACMILLAN EDUCATION AUSTRALIA PTY LTD
627 Chapel Street, South Yarra, Australia, 3141

Associated companies and representatives throughout the world.

Edited by Miriana Dasovic
Text and cover design by Marta White
Maps by Pat Kermode, Purple Rabbit Productions
Photo research by Jes Senbergs

Printed in Thailand

Acknowledgements

The author and the publisher are grateful to the following for permission to reproduce copyright material:

Cover photograph: Adolf Eichmann at his trial, and magnifying glass, courtesy of Getty Images; eye, courtesy of Ingram Royalty Free Image Library.

AAP/AFP Photo, pp. 17 (top), 25 (bottom), 29 (bottom), 30 (top); Asahi Shimbun, p. 9 (top), in *History of the Japanese Secret Service*, by Richard Deacon, Frederick Muller Ltd, London, 1982; Australian Picture Library/Corbis, pp. 17, 21 (bottom), 27, 29 (top); Australian War Memorial negative number 067335, p. 5; Australian War Memorial negative number 067335a, p. 13 (top); Australian War Memorial negative number p01483.001, p. 13 (bottom); Brian Parker, p. 9 (bottom); Bundesarchiv, Koblenz, Bild 101/73/2824/12, p. 15 (bottom); Getty Images, pp. 1, 3, 21 (top), 23 (top), 32 (all); The G.R. "Dick" Roberts Photo Library, p. 25 (top); Ingram Royalty Free Image Library, p. 1 (eye); Mitchell Library, State Library of New South Wales, p. 7; Netherlands Institute for War Documentation, p. 11; Novosti (London), p. 19 (top); Janusz Piekalkiewicz, Rosrath-Hoffnungsthal, p. 15 (top), in *World War II – the Resistance*, edited by Russell Miller, Time-Life Books, Chicago, 1979; U.S. Department of Defense, pp. 19, 23 (bottom); Roy Varner, p. 4, in *A Matter of Risk*, by R. Varner and W. Collier, Random House, NY, 1978.

While every care has been taken to trace and acknowledge copyright, the publisher tenders their apologies for any accidental infringement where copyright has proved untraceable. Where the attempt has been unsuccessful, the publisher welcomes information that would redress the situation.

CONTENTS

INTRODUCTION

Moon Pool was the secret room built in the hold of a spy ship. This room was meant to hide a nuclear submarine.

What is a spy?

A spy is a person who deals in secret information. Some spies gather the information, usually by sly means. Other spies carry the information from one person to another. There are spies who sit at desks and study the information, while other spies go out into the field and act on it. Some spies make up false information and spread it around to fool the enemy. Anyone who works secretly in this way is a spy.

- 👁 The proper name for spying is espionage.
- 👁 The modern name for a spy is an agent or intelligence officer.
- 👁 Information gathered by spies is called intelligence.

When did spying start?

People have been spying on each other since human history began. Army leaders have always known that the best way to defeat an enemy is to find out that enemy's weakness, and the best person to discover that weakness is a spy.

Why do people become spies?

Sometimes people become spies out of loyalty to their country. They gather information that will help keep their country safe. Sometimes people become spies because they know important secret information and sell it for money, usually a lot of money. Some people are tricked or forced into becoming spies. Other people choose to become spies because they find it exciting.

Spies of the early 1900s

In the early 1900s, there were about 7,000 spies in the world. Most of these spies were not trained. They were military officers and civilians who gathered information for their governments. Most of those early spies have been forgotten.

Spies in World Wars I and II

In 1914, when World War I started, thousands of spies were recruited. Many of these spies were trained, but most of them were not trained very well. The best World War I spies were those who had a natural talent for spying. Most of these spies worked alone. This changed when World War II started in 1939. Many thousands of spies were recruited and most of them were highly trained. World War II spies often worked in teams and performed some spectacular feats of espionage.

Cold War spies

In 1945, the Cold War started when World War II ended. It was an era when the United States and the Soviet Union watched each other with great distrust. Each country built up stores of weapons because they expected the other to attack. Both the U.S. and the U.S.S.R. spent a lot of money on technology to help them spy during the Cold War. They built spy planes, satellites, and nuclear submarines. Every now and then something went terribly wrong with this expensive technology.

Today's spies

Today there are hundreds of thousands of spies all around the world. Spies only become famous now if they defect, or betray their country and get caught.

An Australian **commando** spies on Singapore Harbor during World War II.

civilians   people not in the armed forces

commando   specially trained soldier

defect   to switch loyalty from one country to another

into the field   going into other countries to spy

recruited   asked to do a job

Soviet Union   a shortened name for the Union of Soviet Socialist Republics (U.S.S.R.), once called Russia

HERBERT DYCE MURPHY, THE ELEGANT LADY SPY

? By 1900, Germany had built a powerful army.

? The British suspected that Germany was getting ready for war.

Arctic Ocean

England
Oxford
BELGIUM
FRANCE

N

AUSTRALIA
Melbourne

0   5,000 miles

ANTARCTICA
South Pole

Herbert Murphy's first adventure

Herbert Dyce Murphy was born in Melbourne, Australia, in 1879. His family was very rich, but Murphy wanted something that money could not buy. He wanted adventure. At the age of 16, Murphy took a job on a sailing ship. He spent the next four years sailing around the world. One ship even took him to the Arctic, where he hunted whales.

Life at Oxford University

At the age of 20, Murphy went to college at Oxford in England. He became fascinated by trains, and spent hours watching them and taking photographs. Murphy ended up knowing more about trains than the university subjects he was studying. Murphy also liked to act in student plays. In the early 1900s, most university students were men. Murphy was slim and fair, so he always had to play the part of a girl.

One night, the chief of British military intelligence came along to see a play. A week later, the intelligence chief offered Murphy a job as a spy. British military intelligence needed someone to gather information about trains in Belgium and northern France. Murphy was perfect for the job.

Spying in Belgium and France

Murphy knew all about trains. He knew if the running gear on a car was new or old, or if a wagon could carry horses or guns. Many English spies had been sent to France and Belgium to do this job. Most had been caught and sent home. Murphy did something different. To go out spying, he dressed up as an elegant young lady. He wore a wig of long hair, a pretty dress, and a hat with a veil. He called himself Miss Edith Murphy. No one in France or Belgium ever guessed that he was a man.

Measuring the railroad platforms

One of Murphy's jobs was to pace along railroad platforms and measure them by counting his steps. In the early 1900s, all armies moved about by train. A train had to stop at a very long platform to load and unload 10,000 soldiers with horses and heavy guns. The measurements that Murphy took of the platforms helped the British work out which railroad lines the Germans would use when they were ready to move their armies into place.

The end of Murphy's spying career

Murphy had to give up spying after just two years. The hair on his face began to grow too thick to hide. Instead, he went off on different adventures. In 1911, he went to the Antarctic with explorer Mawson. Murphy was part of the team that tried to reach the South Pole.

Miss Edith Murphy and the sea captain, a painting by C. Salis Lloyd, 1902. It shows Herbert Murphy dressed as a woman.

Herbert Murphy in the Antarctic as a member of the Mawson expedition.

KAWASHIMA AND THE BOY-EMPEROR

BACKGROUND

? In 1900, Japan began to build a mighty empire.

? Japan took over Korea and Manchuria, and wanted China next.

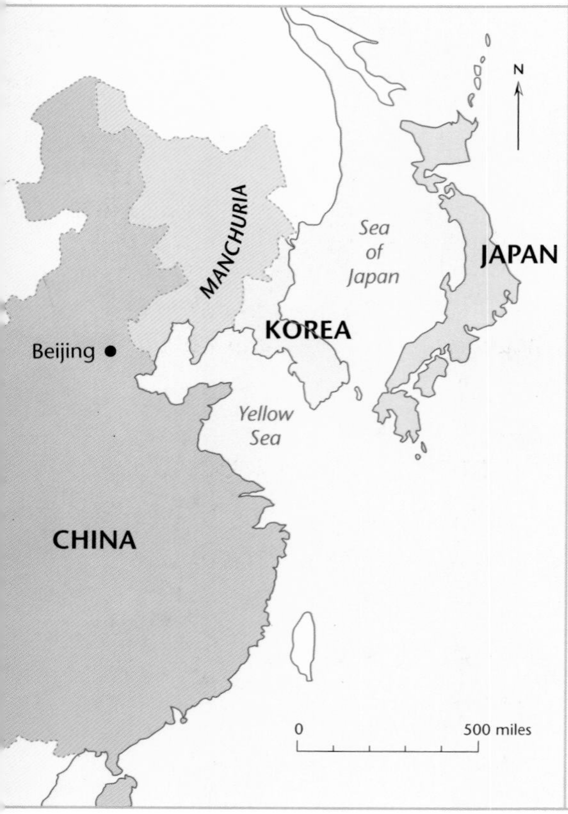

From princess to spy

Yoshiko Kawashima was a Chinese princess. Her father died when she was eight years old, and her Japanese uncle took her into his family. Kawashima's uncle was a Japanese spy. By the age of 15, Kawashima was also spying for the Japanese. To go out spying, she often disguised herself as a boy.

The boy-emperor

The emperor of China was a young boy named Pu-Yi. A new people's government in China had removed Pu-Yi from his throne. This new government said there would be no more emperors. Japan sent a secret message to Pu-Yi. It promised to make him emperor again if he would let Japan take over China. Pu-Yi did not like this plan.

Kawashima goes on a secret mission

Pu-Yi and Kawashima were relatives. One time, Kawashima went to visit young Pu-Yi. She was really there on a secret mission for the Japanese. It was her job to make Pu-Yi change his mind about the Japanese plan. Kawashima told Pu-Yi that his own people, the Chinese, were plotting to kill him. The Japanese, she said, would look after Pu-Yi and keep him safe if he would leave China and go to Manchuria. Pu-Yi did not want to go to Manchuria. He wanted to live in his beautiful palace in the Forbidden City in Beijing. He thought Manchuria was dull.

Map labels: MANCHURIA, Sea of Japan, JAPAN, KOREA, Beijing, Yellow Sea, CHINA, N, 0, 500 miles

Kawashima tricks the emperor

One night, Kawashima sneaked into Pu-Yi's room and put snakes in his bed. A little while later, when Pu-Yi went to climb between the sheets, Kawashima called out "Snake!" She pulled him back. Guards rushed in and killed the snakes. Pu-Yi thought Kawashima had saved his life.

A few days later, Kawashima hid two bombs in a fruit bowl. As Pu-Yi was about to reach for a piece of fruit, Kawashima cried out again just in time to save his life. Kawashima told Pu-Yi that the snakes and the bombs had been hidden there by the Chinese. She urged him to flee to Manchuria. There his friends, the Japanese, would keep him safe. Pu-Yi still would not go.

Kawashima's last plan

Kawashima finally paid a group of Chinese men to attack the soldiers guarding Pu-Yi's house. The fight was very loud and looked very real. It terrified the boy-emperor. He let Kawashima hide him in the trunk of a car. He thought she was saving his life again as she drove away at top speed. Kawashima drove to the docks. There the boy-emperor was taken out of the trunk of the car and quickly put onto a waiting ship. It immediately sailed for Manchuria. For her part in this very successful spy case, Kawashima was made a commander in the Japanese army.

Kawashima disguised as a boy.

The emperor's palace in Beijing was called the Forbidden City because ordinary people were forbidden to enter it. The emperor was believed to be a god, and only special people were allowed to come near him or even look at him.

disguised when a person's appearance is changed so they look like someone else

empire a large number of countries ruled by one powerful country

mission a special job

THE VENLO TRICK

BACKGROUND

? Holland is a small country next to Germany. It is now called the Netherlands.

? In World War II, Holland remained neutral. This meant that it did not take sides in the war.

? Holland was used as a spy base for both sides.

A secret message from Germany

In October 1939, a British spy chief in Holland got a secret message from a German agent. It asked him to meet with an unnamed German general. The message claimed that the German general was plotting to overthrow Hitler and the Nazis. The general wanted to know if the British would help. This was an important message. It could mean a quick and easy end to the war.

Two British spy chiefs, Captain Best and Major Stevens, took charge of the case. They asked the German agent to meet with them. He agreed, and even drove 93 miles (150 km) into Holland to meet with Best and Stevens at The Hague. The British spy chiefs were disappointed when the German agent arrived. They had expected the general to come too.

The German agent said they needed a safer plan before the general could risk a meeting with them. The British spy chiefs agreed to meet with the general in Venlo. This was a town on the border of Holland and Germany. The British spy chiefs wanted to know the general's name, but the German agent refused to tell them.

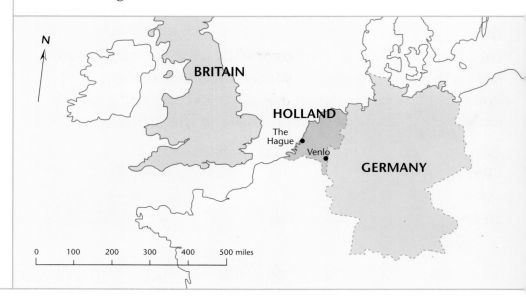

The meeting in Venlo

Captain Best was suspicious of the German agent, but Major Stevens was sure that the man was telling the truth. Stevens was thrilled to be part of this important mission. On November 9, Best and Stevens drove to Venlo. The meeting was to take place in the parking lot of the Café Bachus. The German border was just one block away. As Best and Stevens drove past the café, the German agent stepped out the door and waved to them. This signaled that everything was okay. The British spy chiefs parked in the parking lot. The next minute, they heard a loud roar.

Captain Best (left) and Major Stevens (right).

The Café Bachus in Venlo, Holland.

The snatch

A big black car sped across the German border. Men with machine guns clung to the sides of the car, firing shots into the air. People on the street dived for cover. The black car sped into the parking lot. The two spy chiefs did not have time to run. The gunmen grabbed them and pushed them into the car's back seat. The car sped backwards down the street, its tires screeching as it reversed the way it had come, into Germany. In just a few minutes, the German secret service had caught two top British agents.

Best and Stevens were questioned. Stevens told the Germans everything they wanted to know. A few days later, the Germans shut down the whole British spy ring in Holland.

Nazis   a brutal political and military group that governed Germany from 1933 to 1949

secret service   another name for a spy network

spy ring   a groups of spies working together

THE SECRET VOYAGE OF THE *KRAIT*

BACKGROUND

- In World War II, Japanese forces held most of the islands north of Australia.

- Singapore Island was the most important because the ships of the Japanese navy sheltered there in Singapore Harbor.

Ten Australian commandos

On September 2, 1943, an old Japanese fishing boat left Exmouth on Australia's west coast. The boat was called the *Krait*. Under the old decks there was a brand new engine. On board were 10 Australian soldiers. These men had darkened their skin by rubbing dye into it. They wore straw hats and wrap-around sarongs to disguise themselves as Malay fishermen. They were really army commandos setting out on a daring mission.

The lights of Singapore

The *Krait* sailed north for 17 days until it was 994 miles (1,600 km) inside enemy waters. The commandos were close enough to Singapore to see the sparkling lights of the town. They lowered three small canoes into the water. Two men got into each canoe and paddled towards one of three islands nearby. These islands were tiny and no one lived on them. The *Krait* sailed away. Each canoe landed on a different island, and the men rested until sunset the following day. Then they put on black clothes, got into their canoes, and set off through the darkness, paddling towards Singapore's twinkling lights.

Voyage of the *Krait*

SINGAPORE

SUMATRA

AUSTRALIA

Exmouth

0   500   1,000 miles

N

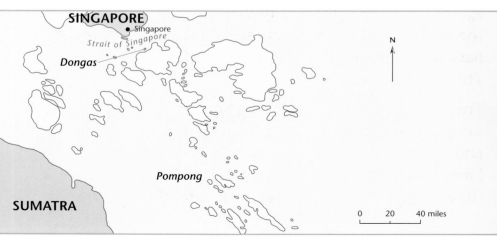

SINGAPORE
• Singapore
Strait of Singapore
Dongas

Pompong

SUMATRA

N

0   20   40 miles

The canoes enter Singapore Harbor

Two hours later, the six commandos were paddling across Singapore Harbor itself. The night was dark. A few Japanese patrol boats moved between the warships. Everything was quiet. Each canoe headed towards a different Japanese ship. The commandos' job was to put mines against the ships' hulls.

One of the canoes was almost run down by a big tugboat in the dark. The team in the second canoe had to paddle right up to a wharf to lay their mines. A Japanese soldier on guard duty seemed to look right at them. However, he did not see them in the dark.

The team in the third canoe was fixing a mine to the hull of a ship when the porthole above them was opened. A Japanese face looked down. There was nothing the commandos could do. They got on with the job of setting the mine and paddled away. Once again, the darkness hid them.

Mission complete

When all the mines were set, the men paddled out to sea again. They reached the tiny island of Dongas just before the mines fixed to the Japanese ships began to explode. Back in Singapore, the harbor was rocked with explosions. Thick smoke rose into the sky.

The commandos rested the next day, then paddled all night until they reached Pompong Island. The *Krait* met them there and returned them safely to Exmouth. The Japanese did not know whom to blame for this attack. The secret mission of the *Krait* was not made public until after the war.

One of the commandos hides his canoe in thick jungle.

The *Krait*.

mines   bombs that are triggered to blow up a certain time after they are put in place

porthole   a ship's window

THE ATLANTIC WALL

What are these strange concrete buildings?

British pilots flying their planes across the coast of France in 1944 started to notice strange new buildings appearing. The buildings were large, made of concrete, and located near beaches. The British needed to know what these buildings were. They wanted to land large armies on the beaches of Belgium and France. First, they needed to know what stood in their way.

The British ask for help

The British asked the French Underground spy network to get a good look at these buildings. Some clever French spies got jobs as workers on the building sites. The spies quickly saw that some of these buildings were forts, and others were bases for very large guns. It looked like the Germans were getting ready to stop the British wherever they might decide to land. This new line of German defenses ran right along the Atlantic coast. It was bad news for the British. They asked the French to get all the information they could about this Atlantic wall. One brave Frenchman found out almost everything the British needed to know.

N

The Atlantic wall

BRITAIN

Atlantic Ocean

GERMANY

BELGIUM

FRANCE

The maps are delivered

René Duchez was a French wallpaper hanger. He got a job hanging new wallpaper in the office of a German major. This major was in charge of building the Atlantic wall. Duchez was in the major's office, showing him wallpaper samples, when a young German officer came in. The young officer left several maps on the major's desk. The maps were long and rolled up, but Duchez could see the end of one. It showed the Atlantic coastline and Duchez guessed what it was—a map of the whole Atlantic wall.

Stealing a map

The major was called to the door of his office for a moment to talk to someone. Duchez looked at the maps. He hesitated a moment, then snatched one up. There was a large mirror on the wall, and Duchez slipped the map behind it. The major returned to his desk and chose the wallpaper he wanted. Duchez left the major's office and walked down the street. He was sure that the map would be missed and the German police would come after him.

Duchez lay awake all night but no police came. The next day, he went back to the major's office and began papering the wall. He checked behind the mirror. The map was still there. Duchez finished work that afternoon and hid the map among his wallpaper rolls. Then he walked out of the building with it. The map Duchez had stolen showed every fort and gun along the Atlantic coast. With this information, the British knew exactly where not to land their troops on the day of the invasion.

René Duchez, the Frenchman who stole the map of the Atlantic wall.

One of the massive German guns used along the Atlantic wall.

Underground   a secret spy force fighting in a country already taken over by the enemy

wallpaper   paper that comes in long rolls and is pasted neatly onto walls

MARITA LORENZ, A SPY FOR LOVE

BACKGROUND

? In 1959, the island of Cuba was taken over by guerrilla fighters led by Fidel Castro.

? Castro then set up a communist government. He also accepted help from the Soviets.

? The U.S. was worried about having communists and Soviets so close to its shores.

Guerrillas on board

In February 1959, Marita Lorenz was sailing around the Gulf of Mexico on a luxury liner. She was 19 years old, and her father was the captain of the ship. As it sailed into Havana Harbor in Cuba, a motor boat came to meet it. Aboard this boat was Fidel Castro, the new leader of Cuba. With him were 20 soldiers carrying machine guns and hand grenades. Castro wanted to look over the liner.

The love boat

Lorenz's father, Captain Lorenz, invited Castro and the soldiers aboard. He showed them around the liner's decks and asked them to stay for dinner. Castro sat next to Lorenz at dinner. He seemed to fall in love with her straight away, and she fell in love with him. Castro wanted Lorenz to stay in Havana, but her father said no. Lorenz slipped Castro a note giving him her address in New York. A few weeks later, two Cuban men knocked at the door of Lorenz's New York apartment. She packed a bag, and flew back to Havana and the man she loved.

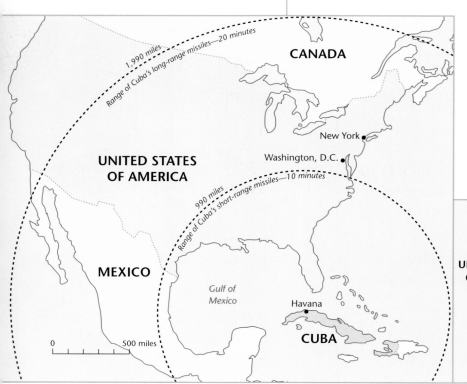

Life on the 24th floor

Lorenz was happy at first. She lived on the 24th floor of the Havana Hilton Hotel. She wore a Cuban rebel uniform and a beret with a star. However, she was never allowed out on her own. After a while, Lorenz began to feel like a prisoner.

One night, one of Castro's bodyguards whispered to her in English, "I'm with the American embassy. I'll get you out." This man was a secret service agent. First, however, he wanted Lorenz to do some spying for him. He got her to look through Castro's maps and papers and take anything that seemed important. A few days later, Lorenz was smuggled onto a plane and flown back to New York.

The Cuban missile crisis

In the U.S., Lorenz learned that Castro was planning to let the Soviets build special bases in Cuba. From these bases they would be able to launch missiles against U.S. cities. Lorenz volunteered to keep on spying against Castro. She flew back to Havana disguised as a tourist, and took a room in a cheap hotel. There she changed into her old rebel uniform. Marita knew that Castro was not in Havana at the time, so she walked boldly into the Havana Hilton Hotel. Using her key to unlock Castro's room, she took as many maps and papers as she could carry. When she got back to the U.S., it was discovered that one of the maps had hand-drawn circles on it. These showed exactly where Soviet missile bases were being built.

Lorenz spied for the U.S., on and off, for the next 20 years.

Marita Lorenz and Fidel Castro when they first met aboard the luxury liner.

Havana Harbor, Cuba.

communist government
a government where voters can elect people from only one political party

embassy   a building where officials from another country work and sometimes live

guerrilla fighters   people who fight in small groups using surprise attacks

THE U-2 SPY PLANE

Super-secret spy planes

The U.S. built a fleet of special jets called U-2s. These planes were built for spying. They had a wide wingspan of 77 feet (23.5 m), flew at a height of 78,740 feet (24,000 m), and carried cameras that took clear, close-up pictures of objects on the ground. The U-2s were kept hidden on remote air force bases, and guarded day and night. Each plane had a special "destruct" button. If a pilot had to parachute out, he pressed this button. It would make the plane blow itself up once he had jumped clear. The U.S. did not want the Soviets capturing one of these planes.

BACKGROUND

- In the 1950s, the Soviet Union started to build nuclear missiles and long-range fighter planes.

- The U.S. feared that the Soviets were getting ready to attack.

- The U.S. had to find out if this was true.

Take-off

In May 1960, a U.S. pilot named Frances Gary Powers took off in a U-2 from Peshawar air base in Pakistan. He was flying above the city of Sverdlovsk in the Soviet Union when his plane's engine stopped. Powers glided down to a lower height where he hoped to restart the engine. Before he could do this, a missile exploded just off the wing of his plane.

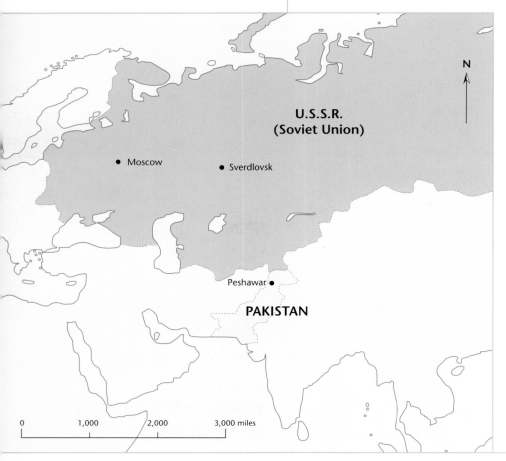

Bail-out

Powers pressed the "destruct" button and ejected from the plane. He parachuted safely to the ground and landed in a field. Powers had everything he needed to survive. He had food, fishing lines, Soviet money, a compass, a map, and more. However, he had not gone far when a group of Soviet farmers ran towards him. They took him prisoner and held him until the police arrived.

Powers told the Soviets that he had been gathering information on the weather when he had accidentally flown into their air space. Powers did not know that the Soviets had found his plane. The U-2 had crashed but it had not exploded. The Soviets had the plane's spy cameras and all the secret photographs.

A display of photographs of Powers and his spy plane was shown to the Soviet people.

The trial

Powers was taken to Moscow and put on trial for spying. He was sentenced to 10 years in prison. The U.S. could do nothing to help Powers or get him out. However, in 1960, a Soviet citizen living in the U.S. was charged with spying. His name was Rudolf Abel. He had been discovered stealing atomic weapons secrets, and was sentenced to 30 years in prison. The Soviets and the U.S. made a deal and, in 1962, Powers was swapped for Rudolf Abel. However, the Soviets would not return the U-2 spy plane.

A U-2 spy plane with its wide wingspan.

ejected	pushed out with force
remote	far away
wingspan	the distance between the ends of two outstretched wings

OPERATION MONSTER

BACKGROUND

? During World War II, the Nazis put millions of Jewish people into camps and murdered them.

? The man in charge of these terrible camps was the German SS officer, Adolf Eichmann.

Eichmann gets away

When Germany lost the war in 1945, Colonel Adolf Eichmann disguised himself as an ordinary soldier and gave himself up to U.S. troops. Some time later, Eichmann was able to get a false passport and slip aboard a ship bound for South America. Eichmann's wife, Veronika, stayed behind in Austria. She told everyone that her husband was dead. Then, in 1952, Veronika Eichmann sailed for South America too. Jewish secret service agents followed her as far as Buenos Aires in Argentina. The government of Argentina protected German people coming to its country. For a while, the search for Eichmann stopped there.

The Jewish survivor

Simon Wiesenthal had been a Jewish prisoner in a Nazi camp during World War II. He was determined to find Eichmann and bring him to trial for war crimes. In 1959, one of Eichmann's old Nazi friends, Doctor von Leer, traveled to South America. Jewish agents followed von Leer. He visited a man named Ricardo Klement, who worked as a factory manager in Buenos Aires. Klement also happened to live with Veronika Eichmann. Wiesenthal guessed they had found Eichmann at last.

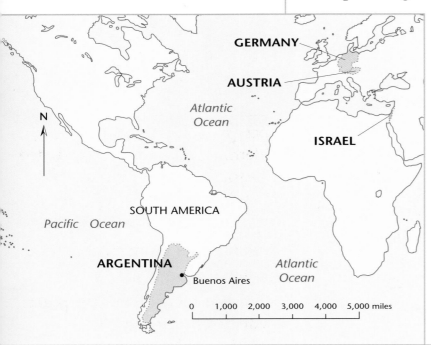

GERMANY

AUSTRIA

Atlantic Ocean

N

ISRAEL

SOUTH AMERICA

Pacific Ocean

ARGENTINA

Atlantic Ocean

Buenos Aires

0   1,000   2,000   3,000   4,000   5,000 miles

Eichmann is kidnapped

On May 11, 1960, Ricardo Klement finished work at the factory and caught the yellow-and-green bus to Liniares Avenue. There he got out and waited for his second bus to come along. Other workers waited at the bus stop too. Klement took no notice of a big black car coming slowly down the street. It stopped in front of him. Four men jumped out and surrounded him. Klement asked them in Spanish, "Who are you?" The men answered in German, "Good evening." Klement was pushed into the car and driven to a house on the other side of town.

Identifying Eichmann

The Jewish agents had X ray pictures of Adolf Eichmann. They had been taken when Eichmann had fractured his skull and collarbone back in Germany. A Jewish doctor now felt Klement's skull and collarbone. Klement had exactly the same fractures. To make doubly sure that this man Klement was really Eichmann, the agents checked the inside of Klement's left arm. Every German SS officer had a tattoo in this place. Klement had a scar where his SS tattoo had been removed. Klement was indeed Eichmann.

Eichmann in court

Nine days later, Eichmann was smuggled aboard a passenger plane at Buenos Aires Airport and flown to Israel. At his trial, Eichmann was charged with ordering the deaths of six million Jews. He said he was only following orders. The court found him guilty and he was hanged on May 31, 1962.

Adolf Eichmann stood trial inside a box of bullet-proof glass because it was feared that someone would shoot him.

The identity card issued to Adolf Eichmann in the name of Ricardo Klement.

passport   an official identification document needed by someone traveling to another country

SS   the *Schutz-Staffel*, a Nazi special police force with immense power

tattoo   a drawing made on the skin with permanent ink

THE RAID ON SON TAY

- In the 1960s, the U.S. helped South Vietnam fight invading forces from communist North Vietnam.

- Some U.S. soldiers were caught during the fight and became prisoners-of-war, or P.O.W.s.

Analyzing spy photographs

United States spy planes flew over North Vietnam taking photographs regularly throughout the Vietnam War. These photographs were studied by military analysts. One day, an expert analyst thought he was seeing things. In a photograph of a small North Vietnamese village, he saw clothes hanging on a line in a military code that formed the letters SAR. This meant "search and rescue."

The analyst studied more photographs of this village. In another, he spotted a pile of rocks laid out in Morse code. This time the message said "prisoners need help." The analyst was sure he had found a secret P.O.W. camp. He ordered the spy planes to take many more photographs.

Rescue plans

The village was called Son Tay and it was 155 miles (250 km) behind enemy lines. A detailed plan was made for rescuing the P.O.W.s. Six helicopters would fly U.S. soldiers into the village. One team would overpower the camp guards. Another team would free the prisoners from their cells. A third team would spread out and make the whole area safe. Then the helicopters would fly everyone out again.

N

NORTH VIETNAM
Son Tay

LAOS

Udorn

Nakhon Phanom

Takhli

THAILAND

SOUTH VIETNAM

→ Son Tay rescue route

○ U.S. bases

0   100   200   300 miles

The models

To help plan the raid, analysts took exact measurements from the photographs and built a tiny scale model of the Son Tay camp. The model showed every hut and tree, even a tiny clothesline. The soldiers making the raid studied this model so they would know exactly what the camp looked like. A second, life-sized model of the camp was built so that the rescue team could practice making the raid. This life-sized model was put up for only four hours a day, and then it was taken down again. The Americans knew that the North Vietnamese were also taking spy photographs from satellites that passed overhead twice a day.

The spy

Three days before the raid, a North Vietnamese spy gave the Americans a list of all P.O.W. camps. Son Tay was not on the list. The Americans talked it over. This spy was new, and he had not given them any good information before. They decided not to trust him. The raid went ahead.

Target—Son Tay

On November 21, 1970, the helicopters took off from three bases in Thailand. Hours later, they landed at Son Tay. The soldiers fought their way into the prison. One team hurried to the cells to free the prisoners, but the cells were empty. The prisoners had been moved to a new camp just 12 miles (20 km) away. The rescue had come one month too late.

A U.S. soldier is taken as a prisoner-of-war by North Vietnamese soldiers.

A scale model of the Son Tay prison camp.

analysts   people who study photographs or reports and work out things from them

code   a secret language

Morse code   signals of dots and dashes that represent letters of the alphabet

THE WARRIOR FOR PEACE

BACKGROUND

- Scientists making atom bombs want to test them to make sure they work.

- Greenpeace is a worldwide group that tries to stop countries from making and testing any more atomic weapons.

French nuclear tests

In 1985, French nuclear scientists planned to test an atom bomb on a deserted coral reef called Mururoa Atoll, in the South Pacific Ocean. Other scientists around the world asked the French not to do this. They said that atom-bomb tests were hurting the environment. The French said that the bomb was harmless and the test would go ahead.

The Greenpeace plan

Greenpeace decided to stop this test in a peaceful way. It planned to sail a ship to Mururoa Atoll. If people were in the test area, the French would have to stop the test. A Greenpeace boat, the *Rainbow Warrior*, was given a new engine and a fresh coat of paint. It was then brought to Auckland in New Zealand, ready to make the journey to Mururoa.

The French volunteer

In April 1985, a French woman named Frederique Bonlieu came to work as a volunteer for Greenpeace in Auckland. She folded letters and put them in envelopes. This woman was really a French spy named Christine Cabon. While helping in the office, she got maps and other information about the *Rainbow Warrior*'s planned voyage.

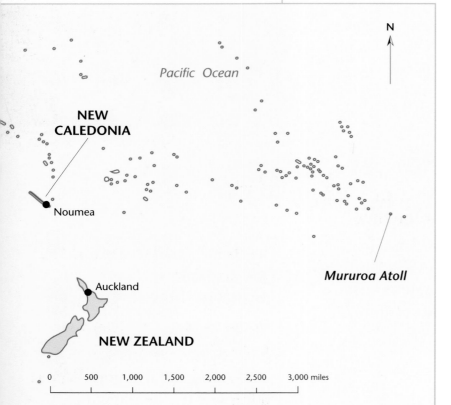

N

Pacific Ocean

NEW CALEDONIA

Noumea

Mururoa Atoll

Auckland

NEW ZEALAND

| 0 | 500 | 1,000 | 1,500 | 2,000 | 2,500 | 3,000 miles |

The *Rainbow Warrior* is sabotaged

At 8.30 P.M. on July 10, 1985, three people launched a rubber dinghy on the north side of Auckland Harbor. They motored across in the dark. The dinghy stopped beside the *Rainbow Warrior*, and two men in diving gear slipped into the water. They fixed a bomb near the ship's propeller and another near the engine room. The dinghy then went east along the harbor and the divers swam west.

Three hours later, the bombs exploded. They tore two holes in the *Rainbow Warrior*'s hull, and the ship sank at its berth. There were 12 people on board, and 11 of them escaped. A Greenpeace photographer, Fernando Pereira, drowned.

The French spies

New Zealand police found the dinghy left on the shore. They then learned that a blue-and-white van had been seen unloading this dinghy. The van had been rented by a French man and woman who turned out to be Major Alain Mafart and Dominique Prieur, both French secret service agents. New Zealand police soon tracked them down.

The French government said it knew nothing about Mafart and Prieur. The New Zealand police next learned that three other French agents had been in Auckland at the time. These three had sailed from French Noumea in a rented yacht. The yacht had left Auckland Harbor the day after the bombing and then disappeared. At last the French government was forced to tell the truth. It had ordered French agents to sink the *Rainbow Warrior* so that it could not interfere with the atomic tests.

Auckland Harbor where the *Rainbow Warrior* was bombed by French spies.

The *Rainbow Warrior* after being bombed in Auckland Harbor.

berth   a place where a ship is tied to a wharf

propeller   a set of revolving blades under the water that push a ship along

volunteer   a person who does a job without being paid

RAISING THE SOVIET SUBMARINE

BACKGROUND

- On April 11, 1968, a Soviet submarine surfaced 620 miles (1,000 km) northwest of Hawaii.

- Without warning, it blew up and sank.

The search is on

When the Soviet submarine sank, it was carrying nuclear missiles and codes used for sending secret messages. The Soviets were desperate to get it back. They searched the ocean where the submarine had gone down, but they could not find it. U.S. navy ships started searching for the submarine too. They found it first. The submarine was lying on the ocean floor. It was still in one piece, but it was 5 miles (8 km) below sea level.

Crazy!

An American scientist working for the U.S. Central Intelligence Agency (CIA) wanted to see the Soviet's nuclear weapons. That meant raising the submarine. People thought he was crazy. They said it could not be done. The scientist was sure it could be. He asked a rich American man, Howard Hughes, to help. Four years later, Hughes and the scientist had built a special ship called the *Glomar Explorer*. On June 20, 1974, it set out to raise the Soviet submarine.

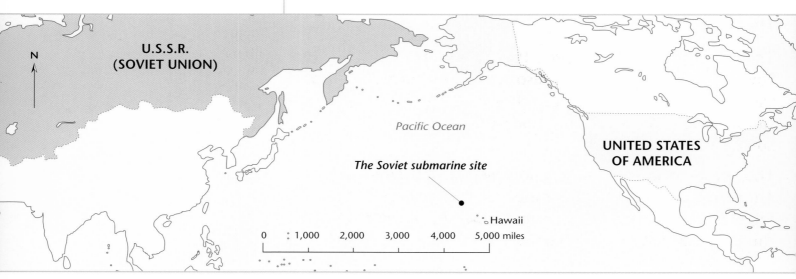

N

**U.S.S.R.
(SOVIET UNION)**

Pacific Ocean

The Soviet submarine site

**UNITED STATES
OF AMERICA**

Hawaii

0   1,000   2,000   3,000   4,000   5,000 miles

A crew of spies

There were 170 men working on the *Glomar Explorer*. Of these, 130 thought the ship was searching for copper, nickel, and other valuable metals on the ocean floor. The other 40 crew members were CIA agents. They knew the ship's true mission.

The *Glomar Explorer*.

Moon Pool

Aboard the *Glomar Explorer* were special things that only the CIA crew members were allowed to see. There was a huge room in the center of the ship. It was called Moon Pool. Its floor opened up. A big claw could be lowered through it to lift things up from the seabed.

By mid-July, the *Glomar Explorer* was in place above the Soviet submarine. The great claw was lowered on a cable 5 miles (8 km) long. The claw's six prongs closed around the submarine. As they dragged against the rocky bottom, three of the prongs were bent out of shape. The claws still picked up the submarine and began to raise it. However, the bent claws could not hold the submarine properly. Just 1 mile (1.5 km) from the surface, the submarine cracked. Two-thirds of it snapped off and sank again. Only the front part was lifted into Moon Pool.

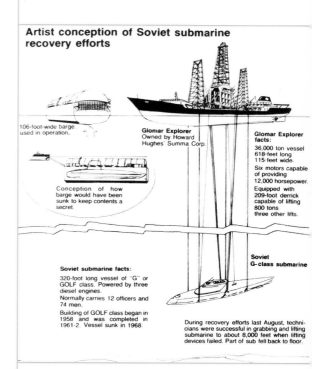

Artist conception of Soviet submarine recovery efforts

106-foot-wide barge used in operation.

Conception of how barge would have been sunk to keep contents a secret.

Glomar Explorer Owned by Howard Hughes' Summa Corp.

Glomar Explorer facts:
36,000 ton vessel 618-feet long 115-feet wide.
Six motors capable of providing 12,000 horsepower.
Equipped with 209-foot derrick capable of lifting 800 tons three other lifts.

Soviet submarine facts:
320-foot long vessel of "G" or GOLF class. Powered by three diesel engines.
Normally carries 12 officers and 74 men.
Building of GOLF class began in 1958 and was completed in 1961-2. Vessel sunk in 1968.

Soviet G-class submarine

During recovery efforts last August, technicians were successful in grabbing and lifting submarine to about 8,000 feet when lifting devices failed. Part of sub fell back to floor.

This artist's impression shows the *Glomar Explorer* lifting the Soviet submarine. When it was drawn the mission was still top secret and the CIA had not given details about the special claw used.

What was found

The Americans found the prize they had hoped for—two Soviet nuclear missiles. They also found four torpedoes and the diary of the submarine's nuclear weapons officer. This simple notebook gave them important details on how the Soviets fired their weapons.

The bodies of several Soviet sailors were in the submarine. They were buried at sea in a funeral service read in both English and Russian. The *Glomar Explorer* is now used for the deep-sea mining of minerals.

THE SACRIFICE

BACKGROUND

? In the 1980s, Cold War tension between the U.S. and the Soviet Union began to ease because the Soviets were running out of money and could not keep on building weapons.

? Because the Soviets could not spend as much money on weapons, they spent more money and time on espionage.

A Soviet general defects

In August 1985, a Soviet general named Vitaly Yurchenko walked into the U.S. embassy in Rome. He said that he wanted to defect. He was the highest-ranking Soviet officer to come over to the U.S. side. The general was flown to the U.S. and questioned for three months.

A list of double agents

By the end of October, Yurchenko had given the Americans the names of several double agents secretly working for the Soviets inside the CIA. Some of these double agents held very important jobs. One was Wu Tai Chin, a Chinese language expert. He had worked for the CIA for 33 years. All that time he had been taking top-secret papers from his office, photographing them, and giving the photographs to the Chinese. The Chinese had then passed the information on to the Soviets.

General Yurchenko also named Jonathan Pollard as a double agent. Pollard worked in the top-secret Terrorism Alert Center in Washington, D.C. He had been selling information to Israel and Taiwan. Taiwan had shared this information with the Soviets. In late November, Pollard and Chin were both arrested.

N

Atlantic Ocean

U.S.S.R. (SOVIET UNION)

Moscow

Rome

Washington, D.C.

UNITED STATES OF AMERICA

CHINA

TAIWAN

Atlantic Ocean

ISRAEL

Pacific Ocean

Pacific Ocean

0   1,000   2,000   3,000   4,000   5,000 miles

Indian Ocean

Double agent Wu Tai Chin is arrested for spying in 1985.

The general disappears

General Yurchenko disappeared one evening when he was having dinner in a restaurant in Washington, D.C. A few hours later, he walked into the Soviet embassy and asked to be taken back to the Soviet Union. Days later, Yurchenko was safely home in Moscow. He was not put in prison like other Soviet defectors. This seemed strange. Nine years later, the mystery of the general's brief defection was revealed.

The dirty trick

In 1994 Aldrich Ames, a senior CIA officer, was caught selling information to the Soviets. Nine years earlier, Ames had been one of the officers who had rounded up Pollard and Chin. It was now revealed that Aldrich Ames had also been a double agent. The CIA had almost uncovered him in 1985. Because Ames was the most valuable of its double agents, the Soviet Union decided to sacrifice other agents to save him. That is why General Yurchenko had pretended to defect, giving away the names of some other double agents. The CIA did not investigate Ames because, after the general's defection, it thought that it had caught all the Soviet spies.

Ames continued spying for another nine years and passed on more secret information than any spy in American history. He betrayed 30 other agents and revealed 100 secret intelligence missions. For this he was paid $2.7 million. Ames is now serving life imprisonment.

Aldrich Ames will spend the rest of his life in a maximum-security prison.

double agents spies pretending to work for one country while secretly working for another

sacrifice give up something valuable in the hope of gaining something more valuable

OPERATION OLYMPICS

BACKGROUND

? Every four years, athletes from around the world compete at the Olympic Games.

? Some of these athletes have been attacked by people who are enemies of their country.

Sydney's nuclear power plant at Lucas Heights.

closed court a trial that is not open to the public

security operation a plan to keep people safe

Sydney 2000 Olympic Games

The Sydney 2000 Olympic Games were the biggest security operation ever held in Australia. Australian Security Intelligence Organisation (ASIO) agents worked behind the scenes, watching and guarding all the visiting presidents and prime ministers. They did this 24 hours a day. ASIO agents also searched the Olympic Games sites every day, looking for bombs or for people acting suspiciously. ASIO did not have enough agents to do all these jobs. It had to recruit 4,000 officers from the Australian army, navy, and air force to help. These men and women were already trained in intelligence work.

During the Sydney Olympic Games, ASIO agents found and got rid of four "suspicious items." They also discovered 57 people who were planning to do something violent during the Olympics. In New Zealand, ASIO agents helped New Zealand police arrest a group of people who were carrying drawings of Sydney's nuclear power plant at Lucas Heights. These people were tried in a closed court. Their names and nationalities have not been revealed. This matter was so top-secret that ASIO still refuses to say who these people are or what they planned to do.

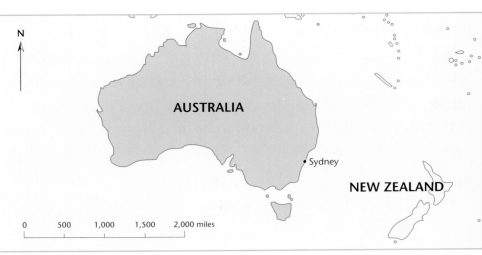

N

AUSTRALIA

• Sydney

NEW ZEALAND

| 0 | 500 | 1,000 | 1,500 | 2,000 miles |

GLOSSARY

analysts   people who study photographs or reports and work out things from them

berth   a place where a ship is tied to a wharf

civilians   people not in the armed forces

closed court   a trial that is not open to the public

code   a secret language

commando   specially trained soldier

communist government   a government where voters can elect people from only one political party

defect   to switch loyalty from one country to another

disguised   when a person's appearance is changed so they look like someone else

double agents   spies pretending to work for one country while secretly working for another

ejected   pushed out with force

embassy   a building where officials from another country work and sometimes live

empire   a large number of countries ruled by one powerful country

guerrilla fighters   people who fight in small groups using surprise attacks

into the field   going into other countries to spy

mines   bombs that are triggered to blow up a certain time after they are put in place

mission   a special job

Morse code   signals of dots and dashes that represent letters of the alphabet

Nazis   a brutal political and military group that governed Germany from 1933 to 1949

passport   an official identification document needed by someone traveling to another country

porthole   a ship's window

propeller   a set of revolving blades under the water that push a ship along

recruited   asked to do a job

remote   far away

sacrifice   give up something valuable in the hope of gaining something more valuable

secret service   another name for a spy network

security operation   a plan to keep people safe

Soviet Union   a shortened name for the Union of Soviet Socialist Republics (U.S.S.R.), once called Russia

spy ring   a groups of spies working together

SS   the *Schutz-Staffel*, a Nazi special police force with immense power

tattoo   a drawing made on the skin with permanent ink

Underground   a secret spy force fighting in a country already taken over by the enemy

volunteer   a person who does a job without being paid

wallpaper   paper that comes in long rolls and is pasted neatly onto walls

wingspan   the distance between the ends of two outstretched wings

INDEX